CB

A very special cat

by Anita Mulvey

New Website
anitamulvey.com

CB A very special cat
by Anita Mulvey

This book was first published in Great Britain in paperback during November 2023.

The moral right of Anita Mulvey is to be identified as the author of this work and has been asserted by her in accordance with the Copyright, Designs and Patents Act of I988.

All rights are reserved, and no part of this book may be produced or utilized in any format, or by any means, electronic or mechanical, including photocopying, recording or by any information storage or retrieval system, without prior permission in writing from the publishers - Coast & Country/Ads2life. ads2life@btinternet.com

All rights reserved.
Copyright © November 2023Anita Mulvey

ISBN: 979-8867683474

Prologue

Let me start by introducing myself. My friends call me CB – and you can too, as I just **know** that we are going to become good friends. I was actually named Cedric-Balthazar by my rather, um, **interesting** parents, but who would want to be saddled with that long mouthful? Certainly not me, so I have been known simply as CB since I first learned to walk on my four paws. Only my grandmother calls me Cedric and I just have to grin and bear it as even she can't manage both halves of my real name.

So that's dealt with that. What else do you need to know? Shall I tell you that I am an extremely handsome, black cat? I am a Manx cat which means that I am naturally perfect without a tail. My eyes are a striking, emerald green and my paws and the very tips of my ears are as white as snow. Surely you can see all that for yourself? But what you won't know yet is that I am certainly one of the cleverest cats in the kingdom. Oh yes - read on, dear friend, and you will soon discover that it is true.

As usual, I instructed my humans to give me my breakfast – oh, I didn't use words, of course, I just jumped on their bed and paddled their chins with my paws until they obey! Then I settled down for a nap as my people set off to work - they need to earn the money to pay for my cat food, don't they?

So far, is this what you were expecting?

But after my doze, I awoke feeling refreshed and ready to start my own work. What do I do, you ask? Just wait and see!

Chapter 1

I collected my hessian sack with my tools in it and set off immediately for the posh-looking house on Finch Crescent. Once there, I slinked into their back garden, not pausing to admire their dolphin fountains or Japanese-style tea house. Gritting my teeth to hold my sack in place over one shoulder, I shimmied up the drainpipe, tiptoed along the fancy parapet on the edge of the roof, then dropped down into the house through the open bathroom window. So handy that the humans had left that window open to clear away the steam after their showers. If only people would groom themselves as we cats do, their homes would certainly be much more secure.

Leaving the bathroom, I padded along the snazzy, octagonal landing to the master bedroom. I knew from my previous reconnaissance visit that there was a massive oil painting on the wall. It was quite good with a beautiful mermaid on a rock, combing her long, seaweedy hair, but I really wasn't interested in the picture itself. Have you worked out yet what I was up to?

Placing my sack on the soft, plush carpet, I reached up and slid the painting sideways a little. Then a brass lever appeared, allowing the picture to swing right out from the wall. I knew that this would happen, as I had seen the homeowners do this when I was watching carefully from my hiding place under their massive bed.

Next, I took my lock-picks out of my sack and set to work, twiddling them most carefully to open the safe. There are almost certainly no safe-crackers as skilled as me on the continent, so I soon heard the satisfying click as the safe swung open.

Nimbly, I jumped right up and into the safe. I knew that there was a square, red box with a diamond necklace inside, so I located that first. Gripping it gently in my mouth, I jumped down and placed it in my sack with my lock-picks and other tools. There was still plenty of room in my sack so it easily doubled up as my swag-bag. Then I returned to the safe. Soon, the matching diamond earrings were in my sack along with an emerald bracelet, a set of gold and platinum cuff links and a rather stunning brooch decorated with rubies, sapphires and pink diamonds. There was also a mysterious, large envelope with a red wax seal. I had no idea what this could be, but I took it anyway.

Then I carefully wiped the safe before closing it. I pulled the painting back into place, remembering to dust my paw-prints off the brass lever and picture frame. It wouldn't be smart to leave clues behind which could identify me, would it?

Swinging my swag-bag over my shoulder and gripping the top in my teeth again, I left the house through the bathroom window. Soon I was confidently trotting away back to my own home. I felt mightily pleased with myself and my haul.

Chapter 2

I sold all the jewels to my usual buyer and I was overjoyed with how much money they raised. She wasn't much interested in the envelope, so I stashed that away for now in my hiding place in our garden shed.

But here is the really good bit – what do you think I did with my ill-gotten gains? No idea? Shall I tell you? I sent it all to the Balthazar Foundation for Orphan Kittens. What do you make of that?

Oh yes, I know that it's **technically** wrong to steal, but I see myself as a modern-day, feline Robin Hood!

I pride myself on staking out my potential robberies most carefully, only stealing from rich people and never from the poor. My crimes are many, but some of my victims don't even notice that they've been robbed. Some humans have so many valuables that they simply think that they have **lost** things. Amazing, but true.

At home after an extremely busy but successful day, I settled down in an armchair for a much-needed and well-deserved rest.

I was snoozing happily when my humans came home. I opened one of my gorgeous, emerald green eyes and was pleased to see that they had bulging bags with them – it wouldn't do to run out of cat food, would it?

"Oh look, Lazybones is asleep. I bet CB has done nothing all day!" they said, laughing.

What a cheek! I gave them both a stink-eye blink and returned to sleep, ready to spring awake when they put my supper in my dish.

I suppose I should introduce my humans to you. I live with Lorna and Nick Lockton. Lorna is an estate agent and is rather pretty with blond, curly hair and blue eyes. Nick works in a bank and is quite tall, rather bald with grey eyes. Of course, neither of them has any idea that I am secretly among the best feline felons in the Western world.

Chapter 3

My next foray of stealth was to a rather palatial bungalow in Salmon Way. On my reconnaissance visit (I had a perfect view into the property from the cherry tree by their back window), I had observed the rather foxy-looking man putting a couple of gold coins in a coffee canister in their kitchen. People do sometimes keep their valuables in the strangest of places.

It was a simple matter for me to slip indoors while the foxy man and his wife were gardening. Carelessly, they had left their back door open so I didn't even need to scale any drainpipes. In a matter of seconds, I had the contents of that coffee tin in my swag-bag and was sauntering happily away before they had even pruned their first rose bush. Back home I examined my filthy lucre and found that I had eleven gold coins and a couple of silver ones for good measure. I was satisfied that some needy kittens would be well-fed with these.

But I couldn't stop there. After a well-deserved 40 winks, I set off for Station Hill. I had spotted a flash sports car in the driveway of number six, so I was pretty confident that there might be some lovely loot in the house. I crept round the garden and was overjoyed to discover a cat flap in the back door. Whist that made for easy access, I needed to establish which cat lived there and what his or her routine was. After all, the chief four-legged filcher in the Northern hemisphere doesn't want to get caught by humans *or* other felines, do they?

So, I took up a good position under a helpful lavender bush and kept watch for a while. No cat appeared, so I risked a sneaky peak in the property. There were no signs of a cat: no dishes of food and no water bowls. There weren't even any traces of fur anywhere. Perhaps the cat and its humans had lived in this house before the present owners. Good news for me, anyway.

I just had time to admire a fancy clock on the mantlepiece when I heard the roar of an engine. In a flash I dashed through the cat flap and sped away before a woman with long, brown hair had even got out of her sports car. I would definitely return when the coast was clear. That clock would provide very nicely for my Foundation's orphans.

Chapter 4

The clock did indeed fetch a great price, and my fence was pleased with the little horse ornament which had also been on the mantlepiece in number 6, Station Hill. No, I haven't gone suddenly mad – the fence in question wasn't the wooden, garden kind but a rather sweet, old lady who often bought my filched treasures. She was a perfect buyer of stolen items as the local police never suspected her for even a second.

So, what next? Of course, I needed to do some careful surveillance around my neighbourhood for my next 'projects'. I was strolling along Chester Street when a perfect opportunity presented itself. The man in number 72 was taking delivery of a very big parcel. While he was busy signing the receipt,

I scooted in quite unnoticed through the open front door.

I found myself in a large hallway and darted upstairs when the homeowner was struggling to get his bulky package indoors. There was nothing much of interest in the study, nor any potential pickings in the spare bedroom. The main bedroom, however, looked promising. There was a fancy dressing table which had an old-fashioned hairbrush, comb and hand mirror in pride of place on the top. A quick examination revealed that these items were made from sterling silver, so I unfastened my emergency swag-bag from around my back paw and stashed the goodies carefully inside. Sometimes, I don't need a second visit to accomplish my goals. There was also a silver trinket box, so I purloined that too. I'd examine its contents later in the safety of my garden shed.

But now I had a potential problem, didn't I? Almost all of my best robberies occur when the homeowners are not there. However, this wasn't the case today, was it? I was just wondering whether I should put the booty back and return for it when no-one was about, when a bit of good luck came my way. The doorbell rang and I heard the newcomer saying that she had come to read the electricity meter. Perfect! As the humans were occupied with that, I sneaked down the stairs and made my escape through the open front door. Careless humans are often my best 'accomplices' without even knowing it.

Back home, I reviewed my takings and was impressed with the quality of the dressing table set. But even better were the contents of the silver trinket box. I found a gold brooch shaped like a dolphin, with some pretty diamonds forming the waves around it. Not only that, but a gold ring with one of the biggest sapphires I had ever seen. As I stashed my spoils in my hiding place in the shed, I congratulated myself that these would provide some necessary shelter for my little moggies. Fortune favours the brave, they say, and I'm delighted that my efforts help so many needy kittens.

Chapter 5

I was casually ambling along Water View the following day and paused to admire a tiny, blue butterfly fluttering over a clump of orange marigolds. Cleverly resisting the urge to chase the little insect, my attention was suddenly snagged by a man heading towards me. He was wearing a smart, pin-striped suit with a contrasting red tie and his polished shoes gleamed in the sunlight. Potential here, I thought.

As he drew level with me, I looked up and purred most invitingly. I waited with bated breath for a moment or two before my cunning plan succeeded. Yes, the man bent down and stroked me and even went so far as to tickle me under my chin. I enjoyed his attention but was not distracted by it, for I had spotted my next 'assignment': a fancy, emerald-encrusted, gold watch around the wrist of my admirer.

The man straightened and set off at once in the direction of Waferside. You may not have visited it, but I knew that there were some very swish homes here, the sort of flats which are not flats but 'apartments'. And I was proved right as my target entered a code into the key pad on the main door and went into the impressive building.

I have made reconnaissance visits before – to 'recce' the place, as we in the trade call it – so I knew that there were five floors with only one huge apartment on each. There was also a basement with a gym and swimming pool for the use of all the residents, although most of them never seemed to bother. I watched as the man opened his brass post box (far too grand to be a simple 'pigeon-hole'), took his letters and made for the lift. He was so intent on his mail that he didn't spot the most intelligent moggy in the world creep into the lift too.

He got out of the lift on the third floor, but I didn't. I had all the information I needed for now and would return with the tools of my trade. I smiled to myself as the lift doors closed and the lift automatically returned to the ground floor, the doors opening ready to receive the next resident to come home. Whoever had programmed this system had not considered how useful it would be to feline felons.

Chapter 6

After that, I scampered home as I wanted to be there before my humans came back, hopefully with some tasty fresh fish for my tea. I settled down on the sofa for some much-deserved shut-eye and was enjoying a lovely dream about a large mouse wearing a valuable gold watch when they returned (sadly, no fish in sight).

"Oh look," laughed Nick, "CB is on the sofa where he was when we left this morning. I bet Lazybones has done absolutely nothing all day!"

Lorna laughed too, but I simply gave them both a stink-eye blink and went back to sleep, prepared to spring awake when they put my supper in my bowl. Most humans have no idea at all how stupendously smart we kitties actually are.

The following day found me back in Riverside for my stake-out of the third-floor apartment. I was just settling down for a catnap on the wooden bench in the impressive front gardens when my target ran right past me. Yes, he sprinted away wearing shorts, tee-shirt and trainers, clearly out for his morning's exercise. So lucky for me.

Immediately, I leaped up and slipped inside the entrance before the main door had fully closed. I didn't waste any time lurking by the lift for a human to appear and operate it for me. No, I shot up the stairs and arrived on the correct floor in record time. I hadn't a moment to spare as I had no idea how long the man's morning jog would be.

With my skilled use of my lock-picks, I was inside the flat in a flash. I scurried around and soon discovered the bedroom. My instincts told me that the man wouldn't wear his precious time-piece when exercising and this proved correct as the impressive watch was right there on the bedside cabinet. I placed it carefully into my swag-bag and was wondering whether I could also swipe any other treasures, when I heard a most unwelcome sound. Someone else was in the apartment!

Fearing discovery, I dashed under the bed, pulling my plunder with me. A woman in a striking red-and-white spotted dress appeared and sat on the bed, on the opposite side to my hiding place.

Now, I had several options here. I could wait until she had left the apartment, but that might mean that I ran straight into the man after his run. Or, I could wait until he had come back and then gone out again, but maybe he would be working from home today and not planning to leave at all. Alternatively, I could just make a run for it now.

I liked this latter idea best – we cat burglars are quite fearless, you know. And I knew that this was the right decision when the lady plugged in her hairdryer. With that noise she surely wouldn't notice a particularly clever puss leaving her home.

In no time at all I was speeding down the stairs and heading for the main door. But before I could press the little button to open it, the man returned from his jog. Was I about to be caught red-handed (or should that be 'red-pawed')?

But no. Fortunately for me, he was engrossed in the headlines of the newspaper he must have bought at the little shop on the corner. Unnoticed, I slinked through the front door as the lift doors shut behind him.

Whew – that was a close one! I escaped by the skin of my whiskers but my little kittens were worth the risk. Another successful expedition for super stealer, CB!

Chapter 7

I arrived home to find an unexpected visitor waiting patiently for me. She was seated in the deck-chair in our garden shed and she had some potentially important information for me.

"Ah, there you are CB," she said as I entered the shed. I will call her 'Agent X' as I don't want to reveal her real name to you in case the police get to hear about it. After all, the top cat burglar to be found on Earth, and in fact on *any* planet, needs his trusted fence to buy his pilfered goodies, doesn't he?

I jumped into her lap and enjoyed a friendly stroke before showing her the gold watch I had so recently 'acquired'. Agent X was most impressed and we settled on a high price which would provide so well for my orphan kitties.

"Right," she said, wrapping the watch carefully in a lace handkerchief and placing it in her handbag, "now I must ask you a question. Have you heard the news today, CB?"

Of course, I had not. I had been far too busy with my mission to bother about that. But dear Agent X went on to tell me all about today's headline and the accompanying details sounded most intriguing. Apparently, a wealthy couple had had some precious jewellery stolen, but were prepared to accept those losses. However, there was something else which had also been stolen, something which they wanted back most desperately. And the really exciting part was that they were willing to pay a tidy sum indeed for its return. Do you have any idea what my friend and fence was talking about? No? Well, do read on…

With her words still ringing in my especially handsome ears, I jumped down from her lap. I reached for the battered, old box which lay on the bottom shelf underneath a rusty pair of garden shears. This box looked quite unpromising and nobody had ever suspected that it contained all my prized swag until I had, er, found every item a new home. With trembling paws, I opened the lid. And there, right at the bottom, was a large, white envelope with a red wax seal.

Agent X ignored the rolled-up oil painting, the silver charm bracelet and the gold locket with a curl of hair in it reputed to be from some famous queen. She took hold of the envelope and examined its seal most carefully.

"I think that this is it!" she cried, jubilantly. "You are such a clever cat, CB. Our fortunes will be made with this!"

Agent X bent down and grabbed hold of my front paws (rather awkwardly, as she still clutched the envelope in one hand) and we did a merry jig to celebrate.

When we were both calm again, she sat down and stroked me most fondly in her lap while we made our plans. Soon we had it all arranged.

Chapter 8

Leaving my dear friend to sort out the envelope business, the next morning found me heading for Hazel Grove where I had been staking out number 132. My super surveillance skills had revealed a very interesting lock-box in the attic there and I was certain that treasure lay inside.

As on my previous recces, the family piled into an enormous car – the sort they sometimes call a 'mini-van'. As soon as the parents and children were strapped in, they set off for work and school with a mighty rumble of the vehicle's powerful engine.

Satisfied that I could now set to work myself, I sidled up the driveway, scrambled over the wrought-iron gate into the back garden and paused under a hydrangea bush. No-one seemed to have noticed me, so I shinned up the drainpipe until I reached the eaves of the roof. Here I shimmied up the diagonal edge of the gable end and onto the very apex of the roof. Balancing carefully, I slinked onto the chimney pot and dropped down into the attic below. My stake-out of this home had revealed that the chimneys were just for show and the real fires had been replaced many years ago, so I didn't get too sooty.

At once I set to work with my trusty lock picks and soon heard the satisfying click as the aged fastener of the lock-box swung open. I had no idea what may be inside, but I was amazed and delighted to find an ancient Egyptian papyrus scroll along with a little statue of their cat god, Bastet. Clearly the humans in this house have unusual but most exquisite taste.

I stashed the treasures carefully in my swag-bag then wiped away my paw prints. My plan was to go downstairs and open one of the windows to make my escape. The safety-conscious people here had fitted locks on all their windows, never once considering that a rascally robber like me might easily open them from the *inside*.

Confidently, I descended the stairs but was immediately assailed by the most dreadful shrieking of a siren. The homeowners had installed a burglar alarm!

Quickly I considered my options, though there was clearly no time to fiddle with the window catches as I could already hear the most unwelcome sound of police sirens. Making a mental note to avoid all the properties on the same street as the police station in future, I dashed under a long, fake fur coat which was hanging with a few less glamourous items on the ornate hall stand. And I was right to hide as a screech of tyres was heard in the driveway only a minute later.

From the safety of my hiding place, I watched as the front door opened and two sets of police-issue shoes came into the hall. Obviously, the officers had a key and also the authority to make an immediate search. I froze instantly, but the fake fur was tickling my nose. I did my best to resist, even holding my breath in case that would help. Unfortunately, not. Just as the first police officer entered the code into the alarm panel and the wailing died away, I had the most enormous, loudest sneeze that I have ever had.

There was a moment of stunned silence and then a hand reached down between the coats. Just as I kicked my swag-bag behind a pair of bright yellow wellington boots, a policeman parted the garments. Yes, I was discovered and by an officer of the law, no less!

Chapter 9

Naturally, I am one of the bravest felines you are ever likely to meet, so I didn't flinch and merely regarded the police officer calmly. And his reaction wasn't quite what I expected.

"Oh look, Sarge, it's just a cat," he laughed, leaning down to give me a friendly stroke.

"Well, that cat must have triggered the alarm, mustn't he?" replied the woman sergeant, chuckling too.

I must admit to you that I was outraged: '*just* a cat' indeed. What a cheek! And 'that cat' wasn't much better. Didn't they know that they were dealing with the brightest star of stealth in the galaxy? Clearly not.

But it worked in my favour, didn't it? So, ignoring their insults, I allowed them both to pet me and even went so far as to purr. After all, I didn't want to end up with handcuffs around my handsome paws, did I?

After a few minutes, the senior officer said that they should check over the house anyway, so that they could make a full report back at the police station afterwards. I waited until they had both climbed the stairs before retrieving my swag-bag and scarpering through the open front door. Phew, what a relief!

Back home I congratulated myself on a most successful mission. Never before have the **police** been my 'accomplices' and actually aided my escape. Super snaffler, CB, wins again!

Chapter 10

A day or two later, I visited Agent X and received a very tidy sum for my ancient Egyptian booty. Better yet, she had some news for me of an important meeting she had arranged for the following Friday.

"Do you want to come with me to the meeting, CB?" she asked.

I considered the matter most carefully, taking account of the fact that the original owners of that mysterious envelope with the red wax seal would obviously be there too. But in the end, I decided not to attend. After all, Agent X would be acting on my behalf anyway and I really didn't want to give away my identity, did I? Future furtive adventures might be scuppered if the police learned that it was me who had, er, '*procured*' the envelope originally.

So, we made our plan and I left, totally satisfied that she was indeed the best person for the meeting.

That Friday started out normally enough. I 'instructed' Lorna to give me my favourite cat food for breakfast, then settled down for a bit of shut eye. When my humans had left for work, I attended to my own tasks and successfully swiped several items which would keep my orphans well-fed for weeks.

Firstly, I came across an opportunity almost by chance. I just happened to be ambling along Mountain Avenue when a removals van pulled up in the driveway of number 49. From my great vantage point behind a silver birch tree in the garden, I looked on as work to load the van started almost immediately. I kept watch and waited - we moggies are patient creatures. At last, while the homeowners were giving the removal team a cup of tea, I was able to sneak into the open van and pinch a rolled-up oil painting of a rather grumpy-looking woman riding a magnificent horse. I stashed it carefully into my emergency swag-bag then scarpered as one of the removal men appeared with a chair to put in the van.

"Oi, what are you doing in our van?" he shouted, but I ran off leaving him with a blurry view of my gorgeous black paws disappearing round the corner. As there were other rolled-up paintings which I didn't pilfer, he was left none the wiser.

Next, I strolled down Marine Mews and paused to admire a bumblebee buzzing happily in a fuchsia bush. My second piece of good luck occurred as I looked in the open window of the nearest home. It was a bungalow and there was a little dish on the window ledge which seemed to glitter in the sunlight. Naturally, I reached in for a closer look and found several interesting rings. I decided to take just one – after all, a feline Robin Hood mustn't be greedy, must he? So, I filched a pretty silver ring set with garnets and opals and made my escape without leaving even one pawprint as a clue.

Tired but happy, I went home for a well-earned snooze. My humans returned eventually and after supper, we all settled down for a relaxing evening in front of the television.

And that was when I had a most unexpected but happy surprise, for the main announcement was accompanied by a photograph of my good friend and fence, Agent X!

Chapter 11

Normally, I don't really listen to the news. Usually, I just let the pictures and words just wash over me as I engage in my post-meal grooming or pre-evening doze. But not today. My particularly handsome ears pricked up and I paid attention to the news, whilst keeping up the pretence of ignoring it so that Lorna and Nick wouldn't suspect anything out of the ordinary. So, I heard how my friend had reported finding a white envelope on the pavement near her home. Upon seeing the red wax seal, she had determined that its contents might be important and had taken it immediately to the local police station. There, the diligent officers had taken custody of the envelope, soon re-uniting it with its original owners. Apparently, a careless burglar must have dropped that envelope when making his or her get-away.

"Such a fortunate turn of events for us," a well-dressed, old woman was saying on the news, holding the envelope for all the viewers to see.

"Yes," her smart husband continued, beaming at the little crowd who had gathered before them by the steps of the police station. "This envelope contains the deeds to the castle which has been in our family for over six hundred years. I'm so grateful to have these deeds back so that I will no longer feel that I've let down all my ancestors. After such a long and distinguished history, I am so relieved that I'm not the one who lost our castle!"

And then came the really good bit – can you guess what announcement this happy couple made next? Well, they declared that Agent X would receive a sizable cash sum as well as being allowed free entry to the castle whenever she wanted. Even better, the couple would allow her to invite all her own family to stay in the castle for a fortnight every August. What do you think of that?

My friend smiled most happily at this news, but shook her head at the same time. When the applause of the little crowd had subsided, she turned to the elderly couple with a question which made my heart sing with joy and pride.

"I have no family of my own," she said, "so, could these holidays be passed to my favourite charity instead? The Balthazar Foundation for Orphan Kittens is a most worthy organisation and I'm sure that the orphans would love a holiday in the castle every year."

And so, it was all agreed and I must tell you that I couldn't have been happier. I insisted that Agent X keep the cash reward for herself in recognition of her hard work and also of our long-standing friendship. After all, not only did my needy, young kitties get the most wonderful holidays but also my Foundation received lots of publicity which led to the topping up of our coffers with no commissions of any crimes at all. Such a welcome change!

And what about me, you ask? Well, the all-time champion cat burglar in the universe didn't actually **need** to get busy for quite a while after that, but I kept my tools handy just in case the ideal opportunity presented itself. Never say never again, as my dear old grandmother used to say.

Quizzes

<u>Did you notice all the terms relating to crimes? Can you remember their meanings? Which **three** words have very similar definitions?</u>

Reconnaissance/recce

Swag-bag

Lock picks

Fence

Surveillance

Accomplice

Safe-cracker

Alibi

Stake out

<u>Could you design a 'Wanted' poster for CB?</u>

Remember to include an image of him and lots of details to help in his identification.

<u>There are lots of words for 'have a little sleep', for example, 'take forty winks' and 'siesta'.</u>

Can you find any others in this story and add any more of your own?

What are the origins of the terms 'take forty winks' and 'siesta'?

<u>*Words or phrases with very similar meanings are called **synonyms**.</u> There are other collections to be found in this story – did you spot them?

A reference book containing synonyms is called a **thesaurus**. Peter Mark Roget published the first one in English in 1852 after starting his collection of lists of meanings in 1805.

<u>Did you note how CB's boasts grew and grew and grew?</u>

It you were brilliant at something – real or imagined – could you describe yourself in a similar way?

Have you met Buttons, another mischievous Manx cat?

Follow her fun adventures in this new Collection:

1. Hello Buttons!
2. Buttons in Trouble!
3. Buttons on Holiday
4. Christmas Buttons
5. Buttons Has a Plan
6. Easter Buttons
7. Buttons and the TT
8. Buttons in Love!
9. Buttons Visits the Vet
10. Buttons Saves the Day

<u>You may also enjoy</u> 'Mollie's Manx Tails' (the Buttons prequel),

'The Fairy Bridge Fairies', 'The Wallababies',

'The Really Wild Wildlife Park' and 'Daisy's Days Out'.

Printed in Great Britain
by Amazon